FEARLESS PUBLIC SPEAKING

FEARLESS PUBLIC SPEAKING

◆

THREE SIMPLE STEPS TO OVERCOME THE FEAR OF MAKING PRESENTATIONS

Anne L. Anastasi, CLTP

iUniverse, Inc.
New York Lincoln Shanghai

FEARLESS PUBLIC SPEAKING
THREE SIMPLE STEPS TO OVERCOME THE FEAR OF MAKING PRESENTATIONS

Copyright © 2006 by Anne L. Anastasi

All rights reserved. No part of this book may be used or reproduced by any means, graphic, electronic, or mechanical, including photocopying, recording, taping or by any information storage retrieval system without the written permission of the publisher except in the case of brief quotations embodied in critical articles and reviews.

iUniverse books may be ordered through booksellers or by contacting:

iUniverse
2021 Pine Lake Road, Suite 100
Lincoln, NE 68512
www.iuniverse.com
1-800-Authors (1-800-288-4677)

ISBN-13: 978-0-595-38305-4 (pbk)
ISBN-13: 978-0-595-82675-9 (ebk)
ISBN-10: 0-595-38305-X (pbk)
ISBN-10: 0-595-82675-X (ebk)

Printed in the United States of America

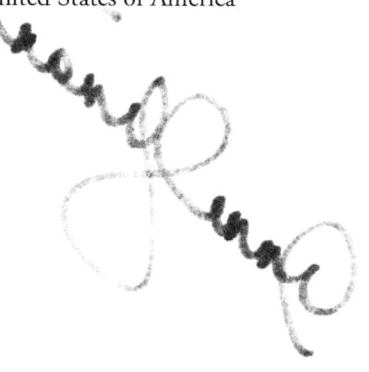

Contents

PREFACE 1
- *Fearless Public Speaking Is as Simple as Learning the Three Ps: Prepare, Practice, Present* *1*

CHAPTER 1 3
- *Using Nerves to Your Advantage* *3*

CHAPTER 2 7
- *You Know All of This, But...* *7*

CHAPTER 3 8
- *A New Era of Speechmaking* *8*

CHAPTER 4 10
- *Step 1: Prepare* *10*
  - Never Assume 12
  - Intelligent, Riveting, and Funny 13

CHAPTER 5 14
- *Step 2: Practice* *14*
  - Talking to Yourself 14
  - Timing 16
  - Talking to Yourself Again 17
  - Use of the English Language 19

CHAPTER 6 20
- *Step 3: Present* *20*
  - The Importance of Your Appearance 22

Warm-up Exercises without Sweat 24
Using Audio-visual Equipment 27
Your Arrival—Working the Crowd…A Little Bit about Meeting People for
    the First Time. 28
Your Introduction 30
A Good Opening. 31
Eye Contact—Where Do I Look? 33

CHAPTER 7 34
- *Working with a Net: Using Slides* *34*

CHAPTER 8 37
- *Business Presentations Made Easy*. *37*

CHAPTER 9 39
- *Unstructured Talks* *39*

CHAPTER 10 41
- *Questions—And (You Hope) Answers*. *41*

CHAPTER 11 44
- *Toasts and Roasts* *44*

CHAPTER 12 46
- *Awards, Dedications, and a Funeral*. *46*

CHAPTER 13 49
- *Gaffs, Blunders, What to Do If You*. *49*

CHAPTER 14 52
- *A Bang-up Ending* *52*

CHAPTER 15 54
- *The Post Game*. *54*

CHAPTER 16 57
- *The Best Ending Story in the History of Mankind*. *57*

PREFACE

FEARLESS PUBLIC SPEAKING IS AS SIMPLE AS LEARNING THE THREE PS: PREPARE, PRACTICE, PRESENT

Many people are afraid of public speaking. They say it is the most feared thing among Americans today. I don't know who "they" are, but because I have heard this statement so many times, from so many people, I tend to believe it. Americans fear public speaking more than the next three items death, snakes, and going to the dentist.

Now think about that statement: People would rather die, encounter a snake, or have a root canal than get up in front of others to give a speech. They would rather die. Let me repeat that: They would rather die! Can you imagine giving a speech in front of a group of ninety-five-year-old dentists in Arizona? Death, snakes, and a drill are just around the corner. In my opinion, all we need to do is get to a level of comfort so that we can get back to fearing the more important things in life, like running out of chocolate sauce or the outlawing of elastic waistbands.

This book will not make light of this widespread fear, because fear is a very personal thing. No one should tell you that you should or should not be afraid because *you feel what you feel*. The goal of this book is to help you reduce that fear or at least help you cope with it.

1

USING NERVES TO YOUR ADVANTAGE

You have heard that great performers typically get nervous prior to stepping on the stage and that it is good to be nervous. There is some truth in that because if you are not nervous, you have probably taken your audience for granted; the audience will know it immediately and they will resent you for it. Butterflies in your stomach and an attack of nerves actually help by increasing your breathing and making you focus. If it were not for nerves forcing you to breathe in and out, you would pass out, and that does not help you in getting your important points across to your audience. And when you are forced to focus you have engaged your brain—always a good thing. So accept the attack of nerves as your wake-up call to focus and breathe.

From now on I want you to rename the feeling you have before a presentation or speech as excitement and not nervousness. When the butterflies dance, dance with them, smile and say, "I am excited, I am focused, and I will bring them to their feet with thundering applause."

PREPARE AND PRACTICE

If you do the first two Ps in this book—prepare and practice—you will have less to worry about when it comes time to present. You will have a plan; you will know the talk backwards and forwards. Much of what makes us nervous is the fear of failing. You can alleviate a great deal of the fear if you know your talk cold! Once you know the talk, you need to be nervous only about equipment failures and laryngitis.

You can also deal with the fear of giving speeches by understanding that the audience is full of people who are also afraid of giving speeches. They are rooting for you to succeed because if you fail, two things will happen:

1. They will feel very, very uncomfortable, and
2. One of them will have to take over…and, remember, they would rather die.

How much more support could you ask for? Popular sports teams have dissenters in the crowd, but you will not. At the beginning of your talk, the audience will be on their knees praying for you to succeed, but by the time you finish this short book you will know how to bring them to their feet.

Whether you are a realtor making a listing presentation to only one person, a CEO making a difficult speech to shareholders, or a sales manager working to motivate your team, the steps are simple, gimmick-less, and proven.

SHERWOOD'S TRIANGLE

A wonderful gentleman, Sherwood Schoch, was a manufacturer's representative who sold sporting goods. Beyond his sales expertise, Sherwood believed that if he trained his customers to be better managers of *their* businesses he would reap the benefits.

Sherwood had a method of sales that he used and taught based on the shape of the triangle. Remembering our schooling, we know that if any point of the triangle is weak, the whole structure collapses. Therefore he labeled the three points with the most important aspects of successful selling:

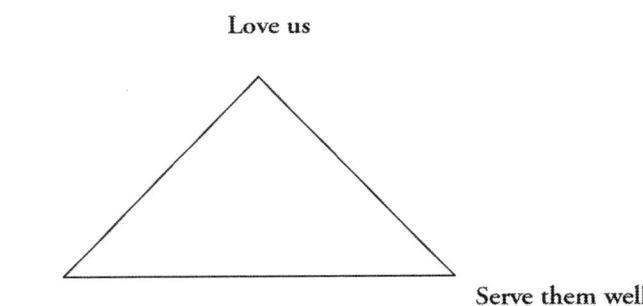

Sherwood's sales triangle reminds us that a customer must "love us." You must be a person or company that the customer respects. You must have integrity, honesty, and empathy.

The customer must also "need us." The customer must think of you as indispensable to his or her business. You are the person who comes through, you are the company with the answers, and you are the resource upon whom your customer depends to resolve their business issues. They need you and view you as a vital part of their success.

They could love you and need you, but if you do not "serve them well," the triangle collapses. Customer service, delivery, and doing what you said you would do are only a few components of serving the customer well and certainly a topic for another time.

The speech or presentation triangle might look like this:

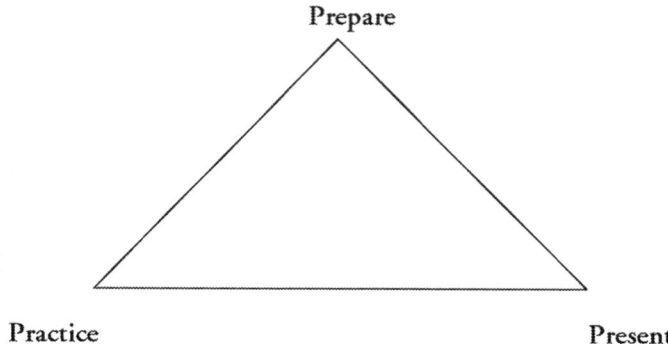

We will address the three triangle points in depth, but you need to recognize and believe that all three points are of equal importance and that a weakness in any one point will not bode well for the success of your talk.

2

YOU KNOW ALL OF THIS, BUT...

There is nothing new when it comes to the techniques used in giving a great presentation. Since you began your professional career, mentors, bosses, co-workers, and family members have given you hints on relaxation and preparation. You have read about eye contact and learned how to put together an outline.

It reminds me of how I learned history while I was in college. I read, studied, and memorized enough information to get me through an exam. I thought I was learning, but now I don't even remember the simple things that helped shape our nation or the details of events that started and ended wars around the world. Of course I remember the major episodes, but the details escape me. Only recently have I stopped blaming my over-cramped brain for my lack of memory and acknowledged that I never really *learned* history; I memorized just enough to get by, only to forget it after I closed my blue book.

You are probably like millions of others who have read or heard about speech-making techniques but never really learned them. You never assimilated them into your brain.

It is time to learn how to give a speech, really learn it, so that the methods become a part of your professional life.

3

A NEW ERA OF SPEECHMAKING

We are not going to dwell on previous attempts you have made at speaking before a group. Larry Weisman of *US Today* (October 18, 2004) wrote about the 5-0 Philadelphia Eagles: "They don't look ahead. They don't look back. They only have today…The Philadelphia Eagles live in the moment, live for this play, this quarter, this half, this game. They savor the incremental steps, the sense of building momentum and the potential for greatness."

This is a new era in your speechmaking life; let's take it one word, one paragraph, one speech at a time from here on out.

Finis origine pendet: "The end depends on the beginning" (Manlius, Roman Poet, 510 AD). This is my favorite quote in Latin, mainly because it is the *only* quote in Latin that I know. "The end depends on the beginning." If at the end of your speech or presentation you want a smiling audience, or a standing ovation, or just an audience that is still awake, you must realize that it all depends on the beginning. I don't mean the actual beginning of the speech, but the work you have done prior to your talk.

To read or not to read (your speech), that is the question. Wrong, it is not the question. You should never, ever read a speech. "But Anne," you say, "I *have* to read my speech because I am too nervous to speak without a script." After you read this book and become more familiar with the steps necessary to calm your mind and prepare your talk, you will not need to read your speeches any longer.

When I watch the president of the United States read from a teleprompter, I have to excuse him (or someday her) for reading the words. If you have to give a different talk almost every day for four or eight years, you would not have the time to prepare and practice. You can bet that the president practices for hours when it comes to the State of the Union address, but there isn't enough time to practice every speech because somebody has to run the country.

But, unless you are the president of the United States or have to give a speech almost every day, you can take the time to prepare and practice.

And if you are the president of the United States and are reading this book, thank you for buying it. (Oh, I gave it to you as a gift; well then, in the words of a great woman, the late Gilda Radnor, "Never mind.")

4

STEP 1: PREPARE

The first step in our simple, three-step process is the preparation for your talk. "Winging it" is not acceptable. It is not fair to the audience that has taken the time to come and hear you; it is not fair to the people who have asked you to speak; and, if this is a sales presentation, it is not fair to you because your livelihood depends on the presentation. This world is moving faster and faster every day and our time is a precious commodity. Don't insult your audience by cavalierly approaching a presentation without preparation and practice.

Begin with an outline of the topic. All good speeches, like all good movies and books, should have a beginning, a middle, and an end. Your outline should follow this premise.

Your outline is simply a guide for your brain. If you are giving a motivational talk or a technical talk, you need to put the information in a logical, understandable order that is easy to follow. Start with the key information and write it down. Then fill in the sub-thoughts you wish to share. As you start filling in the outline, you will undoubtedly think of other things to say, so go back and continually edit the outline. The outline should be fluid and ever changing during this phase.

But it should remain an outline and not a fully written speech. It is your guide, your map, and your course. You will fill in the words during the practice part of your preparation.

One of my favorite authors is Nelson DeMille. His books are intelligently written, entertaining, and, most importantly to me, have a sense of humor. One of his frequent characters is a former NYPD homicide detective turned government agent, John Corey. John is a sarcastic malcontent who finds irony in most everything, yet fights for justice without concern for his personal well-being. He also has no patience for stupidity, carelessness, or people who lack integrity. All and all, he's a cool guy.

In DeMille's book *Night Fall* (2004), John Corey made a comment that I quickly wrote down for future use, "The problem with doing nothing is not knowing when you're finished." If you do not have an outline, if you do not have a map, if you do not have a goal, how do you know if your speech or presentation is doing what you want it to do?

Without preparation, you do not know when you are finished or where you have been, and neither will the audience.

NEVER ASSUME

Not everyone in the audience will have the working knowledge of your topic that you do. After all, you are the one who researched the topic and wrote the outline.

As a speaker I have attended many state and national trade association conventions and often sit in and listen to the speakers who are presenting prior to my talk. State and national trade associations always have speakers who deliver the association's news about legislation, national trends, and industry threats. The speakers are often active in the association and therefore know the background and details of the issues, but sometimes they forget that the audience lacks such knowledge.

Speakers mistakenly *assume* the audience is as knowledgeable as they are, and thus the talks are never detailed enough to make sense to the attendees. Speakers will respond in one of two ways when faced with this fact:

"But, Anne, I have so much I need to tell them, I can't go into detail on every topic." Then you need to cut back on the number of messages you wish to convey. Wouldn't it be better to get one or two clear thoughts across as opposed to none at all?

The second response is: "They should know all about these things, after all it is in the newsletters, and it's just too bad if they don't read them." Well, guess what, the last thing that busy people read are trade newsletters. Busy people are just happy to get through the day having put out the many fires that erupted on their desks. Should they read about legislation that will affect their business? Absolutely! Should they know what is threatening their livelihood? Certainly, but many do not take the time. They rely on their associations to tell them at the conventions, so tell them clearly and *completely*.

INTELLIGENT, RIVETING, AND FUNNY

It is of the utmost importance to *say something*. Just filling in time without content is worthless, and you don't want people leaving your presentation with comments like, "What a waste of time," "I didn't learn anything," "What was she trying to tell us?" I want to walk out of a speech invigorated, smiling, and mulling over what I have just learned. Speeches should be intelligent, riveting, and funny!

When I leave a presentation, I know it was good when my brain has been challenged, I want to hear more, and my funny bone has been tickled. These are great goals for any speechmaker. Obviously, there will be times when you have to make a serious, even dire, speech where humor will be inappropriate. If you take the three elements of intelligence, riveting content, and humor, and change the humor part to human, you will have the components for a staid, serious, and meaningful talk.

Serious subjects, unpleasant news, and unpopular decisions must be handled with a human touch instead of humor. Sincere words must not only be used, but the speechmaker must feel them. Unless you are a great Broadway or Hollywood performer, an audience, particularly an audience that does not want to hear the bad news, discerns insincerity immediately. My advice to you, if you are not sincerely concerned with the news being delivered…ask someone else to give the news.

5

STEP 2: PRACTICE

The second step in our three-step process to better speech making is all about practicing your talk. It is simple yet imperative.

TALKING TO YOURSELF

Once you have the outline, take it to a quiet, private room and talk *out loud* from the outline. Jot down the intelligent things you said during each section of the outline—not verbatim but in enough detail so that you can remember what you said.

Make sure your technical facts are correct, and put them in the outline so that you do not have to pull them from your nervous brain when you are standing in front of your audience. If you are unsure about the facts, either do some research or omit them from your talk.

During this "Talking to Yourself" period, your outline is growing into a speech. If you do not have time to cover the whole outline during this segment of speech preparation, do it a portion at a time. The key is to do this out loud at least three times, jotting notes as you go.

You may decide to change the order or your focus during this first practice session. Don't get attached to any single idea until you have heard it delivered aloud. If it doesn't flow, make sense, or convey the thought you had hoped, you will be the first one to hear it, which is far better than having your audience hear you meandering.

It is difficult to change your mind and start over again on a segment of your talk, but if you are not comfortable at this point of the speech preparation, the delivery in front of the audience will not go well.

I have always believed that it is ok to change your mind because if you never changed your mind, what is the point in having one? After your outline and crib notes are completed, put the talk aside for a day to let your brain rest.

When you are first starting out on the road to successful speechmaking, record your practice sessions on a tape recorder. This exercise helps you determine if you are using words or phrases too often, such as "you know," "umm," or "OK." The use of repetitive words is very distracting to an audience and it draws their attention to the words and not the message.

TIMING

There is no substitute for practicing out loud. Practicing your talk out loud helps you become comfortable and it does something else for you it allows you to time your speech.

If you are asked to speak for an hour, you will not know whether you have enough material if you don't practice out loud and time it. Without knowing your time, you may either run out of material or be only partially through your thoughts when the moderator stands in the back of the room pointing to his or her watch.

More is always better than less, however. If during your talk you decide to skip over a point that was made by another speaker earlier in the day, it is always a good idea to have a few extra notes, slides, or points to use as fill.

I attended a CE/CLE (Continuing Education/Continuing Legal Education) program a few years ago. The program was slated to run for an hour so that the participants could receive a one-hour credit toward their continuing education requirements. A local Recorder of Deeds started her talk, and at the ten-minute mark she said, "Thank you very much," and sat down. The rules are very strict when it comes to continuing education credits, and fortunately we had a moderator who was quick on his feet and saved the day with a question-and-answer period. If you ever run a meeting and doubt whether or not your presenters will be properly prepared, make sure you have a moderator who is talented so that he or she can fill in with singing, dancing, or something to make the audience happy and the accreditation company satisfied.

TALKING TO YOURSELF AGAIN

During an interview on the art of speech making, I was asked, "What is the most important thing you do when preparing for a talk?" That was easy to answer—practice. The key to giving a good speech or presentation is to be comfortable while making it. The audience is anxious for you to do well because remember they would rather die than be up there and they don't want to be a witness to your premature death. But in order to appear comfortable and in control you must

1. Relax; in order to relax you must
2. Know your speech; and in order to know your speech you must
3. Practice.

"We all hate to practice things we're no good at," said Frank Nobilo, a professional golfer in 2004 during a Golf Channel interview. In the beginning you will want to skip this step because you just do not want to hear your inadequacies out loud. Think about it though, all professional athletes practice, and the best among them, Tiger Woods, Vijay Singh and Rachel Hetherington, actually love to practice. It shows in their stellar results. Chip Lutz from Reading, Pennsylvania is one of the finest amateur golfers in the United States and he accomplished this through his talent and his time spent on the practice range. He has said that he could spend hours and hours just perfecting his game and he would love every minute of it. The success of your speech will be in direct proportion to the time you put in prior to the talk.

I remember listening to a president of an organization give an important address to his members. He wandered from topic to topic and back again with no sense of direction or purpose. It is impossible to believe that he practiced his talk or even had an outline for that matter. It was embarrassing when the audience started to shuffle papers and pour water into their glasses. A little practice would have made all the difference.

And here is a simple comment for those who say to me that they do not have time to practice their speeches out loud—don't give the speech, period. Your audience has taken the time to come to your talk and deserve to hear a person who cares enough to give an educational and entertaining speech, not a "winged" talk that wastes their very precious time.

Time is the most precious commodity in our lives today. As consumers we seek to simplify our lives by accomplishing several tasks at once. We brush our teeth and our hair at the same time, hoping that we are using the right brush in the right location. Have you ever tried to get toothpaste out of your hair or styling gel off of your teeth? People treasure their time today because it has shrunk down to very few discretionary minutes. If you waste their time, they will not be happy.

Somebody however has to explain to me how a product can clean the dirt off of the floor and lay a coat of wax down with one sweep of the mop. I don't get it but as time-challenged consumers we want to believe that we have achieved a clean and shinny floor in record time.

You need to practice your speech a number of times prior to the presentation because the talk needs to become routine. You need to be able to get in the zone and you need to allow yourself to get out of the way so that it just happens. This will happen only if you have practiced your speech.

USE OF THE ENGLISH LANGUAGE

Practicing your speech in front of a critic who has a good command of the English language can be very helpful, especially if you are not accustomed to word-smithing. Now, I am the first one to admit that, even though I have a very good command of the rules of English grammar, there are times when I am speaking that two thoughts run together and the result is an improperly phased sentence. As soon as it is out of my mouth, I can hear a buzzer ringing in my brain. My audience has heard it; there is no taking it back so I stop immediately and draw attention to my faux pas. "Oh, that's great English, Anne," I will say sarcastically, and then follow it up with, "but you all know what I mean." Then I rephrase the sentence properly. It will bring a laugh, make you look human, and let the audience know that you realize you made a mistake and aren't too big to admit it.

Swearing is never, ever acceptable. It makes an audience uncomfortable and demonstrates a lazy mind and an uneducated speaker. If you want to be thought of as lazy and stupid, by all means, go ahead and swear. But you were given a brain; use it to come up with another word to fit your thought, even though you think that the swear word is the only word that works. There are other words; there are other phrases.

6

STEP 3: PRESENT

The third and final step in our three-step process is the presentation itself.

PRESENTING—WITH PASSION

Passion, passion, passion. One of our three triangle points needed in unison with Preparation and Practice is Presenting with Passion. Passion comes in many forms, and the appropriate form for any talk is based on the type of talk you are giving.

A motivational speech requires the highest form of passion. Having it and conveying it can be two different things, however. Your motivational talk must convey honest emotions about the topic. During your preparation and practice, make sure you are using phrases that will also motivate you as the speaker (i.e., a tremendous idea, an outstanding method, a world-class product, the best in the business). Believe it yourself and you will convey exciting thoughts.

An educational or technical talk still requires passion, albeit at a less flamboyant level. Your passion will come through in your knowledge of the topic and thoroughness of your presentation of the points. Remember, when you have prepared well and know the subject inside and out, your passion is conveyed when you deliver an understandable talk.

As a salesperson making a presentation, you must reflect a passion about the product at hand or in your abilities to get a job done. Believing in yourself without appearing obnoxious or egotistical is an art, but it is an art that can be mastered. During your practice session, when you are talking out loud, *hear* what you are saying. If it sounds arrogant to you, then it will certainly sound arrogant to your target.

What you say is important, but other factors come into play.

THE IMPORTANCE OF YOUR APPEARANCE

An old adage says, "You never get a second chance to make a first impression." As shallow as this may seem, the sentiment is correct. We have talked about making an impression with your preparedness, content, and delivery of your talk, but we must address your appearance.

You should always dress as a professional businessperson, even if your audience is dressed casually. Unfortunately you are judged by your appearance; therefore if you appear in casual attire your audience will get the impression that your material and credentials are weak. They will view you as a person who has not taken your presentation, or your audience, seriously.

There are many rules when it comes to dressing professionally. Here are some of mine:

Men should wear dress shirts and ties, along with their suits or blazers, in tasteful colors and patterns. Women should wear dresses or skirted suits and can wear pants as long as they are accompanied with a suit jacket or a blazer. The material for both the male and female attire should never shine. And need it be said that all clothing should be spotless, clean and pressed?

Shoes should be conservative. Stilettos are not appropriate, ladies (and, men, if you are so inclined). Your clothes should not shine but your shoes should.

Jewelry—women should wear no more than six pieces and men no more than four (each earring counts as one, glasses count as one, cuff links count as two, etc.). Be conservative, and, if you think that the extra piece of jewelry you are considering wearing may be too much, it is!

And to be very personal, you need to check your hair, teeth, and breath before entering the venue. A quick look in the restroom mirror or your rearview mirror may save you from great embarrassment.

I heard another saying years ago that I use when talking to challenging employees: "You should dress for the job you want, not the job you have." We should make a conscious effort to dress appropriately when preparing for work in the morning or when leaving the house or hotel room prior to a speech.

WARM-UP EXERCISES WITHOUT SWEAT

Warm up…your brain. Treat your brain as you would any other muscle. You know the importance of warming up prior to any activity involving your muscles. Golfers stretch their arm and leg muscles, as do swimmers, football players, baseball players, and racecar drivers. All intelligent athletes spend a significant amount of time prepping their muscles for maximum results.

Our brains also benefit from a good warm-up prior to putting them into motion. If you know your brain is properly prepared to function at its highest possible level, it is one less thing to worry about while standing before your audience.

Athletes always warm up their muscles in order to avoid injury. You ask, "How can I get injured during a speech?" Oh, let me count the ways. If you are giving a talk that includes facts and figures, your credibility is at stake; if you are giving a sales talk, your livelihood is at stake; if you are giving a motivational talk and you mis-speak, your integrity is at stake. Oh yes, you can be injured if the brain does not function well during a talk.

A FEW SIMPLE WARM-UPS:

1. Run some multiplication tables—start with the fives (5, 10, 15, 20, 25, etc.). Fives are easy. Next do the nines, and then challenge yourself with the eights.

2. I like to pick numbers between one and one hundred and try to remember which professional athlete wore the number. (Here are some examples: 17 John Havlicek, 23 Michael Jordan, 80 Jerry Rice, 35 Bernie Perant, 4 Bret Favre.)

3. You could try to name musical bands from A to Z: Abba, Boys II Men, Commodores, Def Leppard. Let me know who pick when you get to X.

Don't agonize over the fact that you did not name every player or complete the multiplication table. These exercises are not suggested to create anxiety; they are merely ideas to get you ready for your speech.

Warm up…your voice. If you are driving to your speech, you already know what I am going to suggest—sing. Turn on the radio, put in your favorite CD, and sing as if you are giving a concert to the Hard of Hearing Society. Do a simple do, re, mi, count out loud, or break into "You've Lost that Loving Feeling" by the Righteous Brothers. Anything will work—just open up your mouth and emit sound. Be careful not to strain your voice; just get your vocal chords ready. A warmed-up voice will also help keep your speech from being monotone or squeaky.

And make sure at the end of your warm-up session you laugh out loud. Laughter always calms me and makes me smile, which is a great way to walk into any presentation.

DRINKING PRIOR TO YOUR TALK

I know that I do not have to discuss the use of alcohol prior to your talk because you are all professional enough to know that drinking alcohol before your speech is just plain stupid. The key to a great presentation is having a fine-tuned brain. You need to be able to think quickly on your feet and to focus. Alcohol consumption dulls the very thing that you need functioning at its highest level: your brain.

USING AUDIO-VISUAL EQUIPMENT

Arriving early is essential if you are using audiovisual equipment. I have never arrived at a speech where something wasn't missing. Something as simple as an extension cord can take an hour to locate, and it is unnerving to arrive just before your talk and have to scramble to find the missing pieces.

You also need to check the equipment to make sure it is functioning. Turn on the projector, power up your laptop, and run a few screens of your slide presentation. Check everything that you intend to use, right down to the microphones and the light on the podium.

A full practice with your laptop and projector prior to your talk is imperative. You can do it in your hotel room, your office or arrive extra early at the speech location. It will be rather embarrassing if you have difficulty with the equipment. Fumbling and the accompanying grumbling can cause the audience to become very uncomfortable.

If you are a person who walks around a great deal during a speech, test the lavaliere microphone in various locations around the room. Certain microphone frequencies react negatively under certain overhead speakers. Know the spots to avoid, unless you intend to use that infernal feedback screech to keep your audience awake.

If you are providing your own LCD projector, always carry a spare bulb. "But, Anne, do you know how much they cost?" Yes I do, having just spent over $400 for my spare bulb, but it is all a part of being prepared to give a great talk. What happens if you are in the middle of your talk and the bulb dies? At that point, $400 doesn't seem like such a waste of money, does it?

YOUR ARRIVAL—WORKING THE CROWD...A LITTLE BIT ABOUT MEETING PEOPLE FOR THE FIRST TIME

Nothing is more important or more unique to a person than his or her name. When giving a talk on customer service, I always talk about the importance of the person who answers the phone for your company. Oftentimes the position is the least paying and least trained, when in fact this person should actually be considered one of your company's most important assets. The person answering the phone can make or break a relationship by how he or she answers, what words are used, and his or her tone of voice.

If the person answering has a nice voice, says a welcoming word or two, and *then* recognizes the voice of the caller, you have won a customer's loyalty.

A good friend of mine, Don Salmon, used to own a mortgage company called Phoenix Mortgage. Being short-handed one particular summer, Donald asked his personal assistant Judy Acker to answer the phones during the lunch hour. Judy would answer, "It's a great day at Phoenix Mortgage. How can I help you?" Whenever you called and heard Judy's catchy welcome, you could not help but smile. She also recognized the voices of many of the callers. She made you feel like a part of the family.

Recognizing and using a person's name is a great compliment, and even during the most difficult times it can go a long way. For example, one day in late June (the busiest time of the year for mortgage closings) I called to see how the folks at Phoenix Mortgage were holding up after a major computer crash earlier in the week. Judy answered, "It's a great day at Phoenix Mortgage. How can I help you?" with the usual smile in her voice.

I said, "Judy, it's me, how are you guys holding up?"

"Holy *cow* [word changed to protect Judy's integrity], Anne, it's a disaster here." But you would have never known it when she first answered. The person who answers your phone should be trained well and paid well.

Whether you are at a business meeting, a cocktail party, your child's soccer game, or walking into your speech, you will invariably be introduced to new people. One of my many weaknesses is remembering the names of people who have already been introduced to me. Years ago, I learned a method to help me remember. When you are introduced to a person, always repeat their name in your greeting.

"Anne, this is Bill from ABC."
"Hello, Bill from ABC, it is nice to meet you."

Now, to help ingrain the name into my feeble brain, I need to repeat it often. But the conversation should *not* sound like this: "Hello, Bill from ABC, it is nice to meet you, Bill from ABC. Bill, do you live locally, Bill from ABC, or did you, Bill, have to drive a long distance to get to our talk, Bill? Bill, what is it that you do at ABC? Bill, where is ABC located, Bill?"

It would sound a wee bit better like this:

"Hello, Bill from ABC, it is nice to meet you. Do you live locally, Bill, or did you have to drive a long distance to our talk today? What is it that you do at ABC, Bill?"

My problem in remembering names is complicated by the fact that I have trouble remembering this advice.

YOUR INTRODUCTION

Most speakers provide their own bios as their introduction. Brevity is the key. Include the highlights of your career that affect the audience you are addressing that day. They don't need to know—nor do they want to know—about your high school athletic accomplishments (unless of course you are addressing a high school athletic association). Your introduction should be short, sweet, and then over.

As you approach the podium, shake hands with the person who introduced you. Ladies, I don't know who decided women should either not shake hands or should shake fingers, but it is *absolutely* horrible when a woman does not have a firm handshake. The webbing between your thumb and your pointer finger should meet the webbing between the thumb and pointer finger of the other person. The grip should be firm, not crippling, and you should look the person in the eye and say thank you.

A GOOD OPENING

You want to make the audience relax, not to the point of sleeping but to the point of comfort. Start with giving thanks to the people who invited you and to your audience for their attendance. A nice comment about the area, town, or state is always appropriate, but sincerity is a must. I remember receiving a speeding ticket on my way to my speech as I left the airport in Indianapolis. I made the comment about how kind the people in Indiana were, since even the police wanted to personally welcome me to their fine state.

If you are a sports fan, as I am, know what the local teams are doing. You could open with a comment about a local player's ERA, PAT streak, or free throw percentage. If you're in Boston, you can always talk about the Red Sox and Fenway Park, or you can talk about local celebrities. I was in Salt Lake City in 2004 during Ken Jennings's reign on *Jeopardy!* At the time, his winning streak was up to forty-two games. I mentioned at the beginning of my talk that I was nervous speaking to the fine people from Salt Lake City because, if they were all as intelligent as the *Jeopardy!* champ Ken Jennings, I didn't stand a chance to teach them anything new. This was a compliment to the people of Salt Lake, which made them feel good and thus warmed them to me before my talk even began.

Once in Las Vegas I quipped, "They say what happens in Vegas, stays in Vegas. Does that mean if you learn something from my talk you won't take it back to your office?"

There is a school of thought that you should open with a joke, but let's just say your opening should make people smile. If you need to use a joke because you can't think of anything with local flavor, be sure to use appropriate humor as discussed in this book. Remember, people like to hear good things about themselves or their towns more than they like to hear a good joke. Just make them smile.

As in any situation, a mood needs to be set. Your goal is to create a relaxed atmosphere. When you make your audience smile or compliment them, they have taken a deep breath, settled down in their seats, and are now pulling for you to succeed. I like to think of my audiences as the hometown fans who are cheering me on. They are my twelfth man and I now have the home court advantage.

EYE CONTACT—WHERE DO I LOOK?

Despite what you have previously heard or read, it is OK to look at people in the audience. If you are deathly afraid, nervous, and quivering you could focus above the heads of the people in the last row, giving the appearance that you are looking at them, when in fact you are looking at the wall in the back of the room. My hope is that once you get more comfortable with giving a speech you can do what I do: find three or four friendly faces in different spots around the room and focus on them. Find someone in the front, someone on the right, and someone on the left. If during the course of your speech you find that they are not giving you positive feelings, then by all means find another person in that general vicinity.

One of my funniest experiences happened in Coco Beach, Florida. I was giving a talk on marketing, and a lovely woman in the audience was nodding at everything I said. In my egotistical brain she was agreeing (emphatically) with every point I made, so obviously my eyes continued to come back to her as I looked around the room.

At the end of my talk she came up to thank me for coming, and I realized that she had an affliction that caused her head to bob up and down. It isn't funny that she had a twitch, but it is funny that I took it as an ardent vote of approval for my words. I still smile today when I remember that my optimistic attitude and ego found her nodding to be such a comfort.

You will find warm and receptive faces in the audience rather quickly, so find them and stick with them. Once you are comfortable with speaking and you would like a challenge, find a grumpy face and do everything you can to make him smile. Extend your eye contact with Mr. Grumpy a few extra seconds—smile right at him. If you cannot change his attitude, don't let it throw you. Smile to yourself and be thankful that you don't have to live his sorry life.

7

WORKING WITH A NET: USING SLIDES

Using slides or other projection tools has pros and cons for both the speaker and the audience. You can use your speech outline to create your slides; the slides then become your guide so that you don't need papers or notes. This allows you to keep your head up and your eyes focused on your audience while catching only glimpses of the screen.

A full practice with all of the equipment is imperative. It will be rather embarrassing if you have difficulty with the equipment.

Your slides should not contain a great deal of detail because it will entice you to read the slide rather than give your talk; therefore, less is better. A great deal of detail also distracts your audience because they will spend time reading the slide instead of listening to you.

If you are explaining a multi faceted-concept or moving from one topic to another, master the transition aspect of your program so that only one line of information appears at a time. This will keep your audience from jumping ahead and reaching your important points prior to your explanation, thus reducing the impact of your words.

I use slides for my presentations whenever possible because I like to move around the room and do not like to be tied to my notes on a podium; however, some problems can arise from the reliance of this safety net.

Even the most diligent testing could not have prepared me for what happened in Michigan. I was giving a very technical speech about the creation of a certain type of business model in upstate Michigan in 2004. We were in a beautiful conference center with all of the latest equipment. I arrived early and hooked up my laptop to the projector, satisfying myself that everything was in great working order and because I was slated to speak third, I chose to sit in the audience and listen to the morning speakers, enjoying their talks. Chuck Kovaleski, the national president of the trade association, gave a warm and fun talk and even paid me a great compliment by telling the audience that they were in for a real treat. Chuck was a great warm-up for me, and after his kind introduction I felt relaxed and ready to dive into the tedious and detailed material.

About a third of the way into my talk, the projector flickered and died, the lights in the room flickered and died, and my heart flicked, but thankfully did not die. All of the power in the resort had been lost; we later found out the entire county had lost power...so now what? The room had large windows overlooking a beautiful mountain scene, so we threw open the curtains to let the light in. While the audience shuffled, wondering what I could possibly do, I looked at them, smiled, pointed to the blank screen, and said, "Now, as you can see in this example..." They laughed and applauded, I took a deep breath and on we went.

The speech had to be changed midstream because I could no longer take them through the financial scenario that had moments earlier been on the screen. I had to speak in more general terms, but the audience understood the concept well enough without the detail. What saved me from panic was my outline. The battery power on my laptop (I charged it fully the night before) allowed me to view the screens thus I still had my guide.

However, I learned a very valuable lesson that day. Always print out your screens prior to leaving your office for your talk. Had the battery power died on the laptop, I would not have been able to cover the topic in as orderly a manner.

The audience was pulling for me to succeed that day. When I joked about how they could have just asked me to stop rather than going to the trouble of turning out the lights, they realized I was going to continue and make it fun. In the beginning of this book we talked about how the audience wants you to do well because they would rather die than be in your shoes: this audience was no different.

When my talk was finished, I looked at them for a few seconds, took a deep breath, smiled widely, and said, "Folks, I hope you are no longer in the dark about these business models. Thanks for your hospitality." I received a standing ovation, and the promoters sent me a rather large bonus.

Lesson learned: charge your batteries on your laptop and take a copy of your outline in your carryon luggage.

8

BUSINESS PRESENTATIONS MADE EASY

Your town's service organizations constantly need speakers to address their meetings, and, if your boss encourages you to market yourself and your company, this is the perfect opportunity. It seems like a perfect opportunity, except you are scared silly. Here is an easy way to promote your industry, your company, and yourself with very little anxiety on your part.

Whether you provide products or services, your company invariably follows a certain process from the time the call comes in to the time of delivery. You are fully knowledgeable of the process, and all you need to do is to convey that process to the audience in an understandable, fun way.

When preparing your outline, write down the major steps necessary to complete the order. Don't get into the minutia, because too much detail equals snores. Cover enough of the topic to educate your listeners. Six to ten steps would be ideal.

Then get a few glossy magazines and cut out 8 × 10 pictures of beautiful people. If they are recognizable people, it is even better, but make sure they are people who are not currently in jail, on trial, or about to be sentenced. You will understand why in a minute.

Take the 8 × 10 magazine pages and put them in simple, self-standing frames, and, as you describe step number one, place the first picture on a table facing the audience. People will not only start to pay attention, they will smile. You then described the duties of the person (let's say you chose a picture of Colin Powell) when it comes to getting the order started.

"When Colin receives the call, he will ask the pertinent questions such as…Colin will then give the order information to Arnold." You then place the picture of Arnold Schwarzenegger right next to Colin Powell. After you describe Arnold's role in completing the order, move on to the next.

The audience is listening, laughing, and anticipating who will come next. Once, when preparing a talk on the workings in a title insurance agency, the only magazine at my immediate disposal was a fashion magazine. I pulled out pictures of magnificently beautiful woman and used them as the staff in my office. By the time my talk was finished, I had ten pictures of some of the most beautiful women in the world. One man commented that if the pictures represented my staff, not only was he going to use us, he wanted to work in our office.

Care must always be taken when choosing the pictures. There are certain sensitivities in the world, and you should never, ever insult, demean, or embarrass people in the crowd. Scantily clad women may appeal to some people, but I for one would walk out of such a presentation. Take the safe road and pick movie stars, politicians, or sports heroes. (But if you are speaking in a town where the local football team lost the previous year's Super Bowl, I wouldn't pick pictures of players from the victorious team…Just a thought.)

9

UNSTRUCTURED TALKS

This may sound contrary to everything else you have read in this book, but there are times when a talk can be very professional even if it is not as scripted as I have previously suggested. It took several weeks of my listening to such a speaker to convince me of this.

I joined Weight Watchers. I would like to tell you that I joined strictly as research for this book, but that would not be the case. However, I can tell you that they almost did not let me join because I only had nine extra pounds to shed. Nevertheless, join I did. The success of the Weight Watchers program does not simply rest with the understanding that if you put it in your mouth it will end up on your hips. No Sir Re Bub! The true success of Weight Watchers is the leader's ability to get in your head with helpful hints and motivation.

We have repeatedly talked about how a successful talk comes from preparation and practice. You have to want it badly enough to put in the time and the work and to forsake other things so that in the end you will have the chance to succeed. But in this program the leader has to stand in front of forty to fifty people eight hours a day, six days a week fifty-two weeks a year, and have enough material to make it fresh.

Luckily for me I had a meeting leader, Andy Auerbach, who could do just that. I realize that Weight Watchers gives Andy the topics to cover, but a script cannot instill her with the ability to motivate a room full of people over and over again.

Most audiences who know they have to do something, but don't really want to, break down into four different types of people: (1) those who are sponges awaiting the gospel of her words; (2) those who sit with arms crossed, challenging her to prove herself; (3) those who have wandering minds and maybe, if they are lucky, will hear every third word; and (4) those who tune her out completely. Andy's challenge as a speaker is to rope them all in with her words and presentation skills.

And rope in she does. Here is what I have observed of Andy's technique. She reaches out to the group with her eyes from the moment she starts to speak. She catches the eye of everyone in the room, which makes the individuals in the group think she is talking to them alone. When a speaker makes eye contact with you and has a pleasant look on her face, you feel special. You feel like you are her favorite and fear looking away because you want to make sure you are attentive when her gaze comes back to you, as you know it will.

Andy also has a tremendous skill that I have never been able to master: she remembers names. She remembers names! Let me say it one more time, she remembers names. A previous chapter discussed the importance of remembering names, and here is a prime example of the value of this skill.

Her talk is not scripted, but it is outlined to highlight certain points for that particular week's topic. For sixty minutes this wonderful speaker looks at you, calls you by name, talks to you calmly, and empowers you so that you know success is inevitable. Wouldn't it be great if within an hour you could reign in your audience, reach them, and send them home with a belief in themselves? Here's to you Andy, and, oh, about those nine pounds, you can keep them, because I never want them back again.

10

QUESTIONS—AND (YOU HOPE) ANSWERS

When you are nervous about giving a speech, any sort of interruption can throw you off balance; thus, someone asking a question in the middle of your train of thought has the potential of derailing your entire presentation. Once you become comfortable standing in front of an audience, a raised hand will not upset your flow.

Early in your speaking career, you may want to ask the audience to hold their questions until the end. But as you gain experience, you may come to appreciate an interruption. Questions naturally occur when you haven't explained a topic simplistically enough. If one person is confused, chances are others are also in need of clarification. Of course, there will be occasions when an audience member just wants to challenge your words. Don't panic—we'll talk about these sorry saps in a minute.

If a hand goes up and you want to finish your train of thought before you answer, just acknowledge the person with direct eye contact and a nod of the head, indicating that you will be with him or her in a moment. Finish your thought then go right to the person with the question.

At times, a question will arise about a point you intended to cover later in the program. You have two choices: answer it briefly and promise more information later or tell the person that it is a great question and that if he or she will give you a few minutes, you will answer it. As I like to make light of most situations, I will compliment the person who asked the question on their ESP, and, when I come to the point in my program that addresses the question, will remind the audience that it is now time to answer our resident seer's query.

IF YOU JUST DON'T KNOW THE ANSWER

You won't know the answer to every question that arises during a presentation. There are surefire methods to handle these situations that will allow you to save face.

First, try to turn the question back to the audience: "That's a great question. Who here in the audience wants to take a stab at the answer?" Often hearing someone else's thoughts on the topic will help you come up with an answer. If someone gives a plausible or correct answer, just rephrase the reply for clarification purposes.

However, if you do not receive help from the audience, be honest and say, "You know what, I really don't know the answer. Why don't you leave me your card, and I'll get the answer and call you."

THE SAD SAPS

I hope this doesn't happen to you often, but there may come a time when an audience member is having a bad day and decides that you should too. This person may attempt to trump you in three ways. He or she may…

- verbally challenge the things you are saying,
- sit in the audience shaking his or her head, or
- interrupt you with his or her opinion and fail to relinquish the floor back to you.

When this happens, take a deep breath, continue to smile, and let the person have his or her say—to a point. Never argue or appear impatient. The audience will catch on and empathize with you, all the while drawing their own conclusions about Mr. or Ms. Sad Sap (SS). If SS fails to run out of steam (which rarely happens), cut in when SS takes a breath and ask SS nicely if you both can continue this discussion afterward. Explain that time constraints require you to move to another point, but assure SS that you can't wait to talk after the presentation.

11

TOASTS AND ROASTS

Toasts, roasts, and invocations are all shortened opportunities for you to make an impression. And because you have only thirty seconds for a toast or an invocation and maybe three minutes for a roast, you need to make every word count. Rambling is unacceptable.

When giving a toast, make sure your comments are all about the occasion and the people to whom you are dedicating your toast. It is my strong, strong opinion that your language and comments must not be offensive. Off-color, racial, or sexist comments are going to offend someone in the room, and, if you want to say something funny, you must not descend to that level.

GREAT TOASTS AND ROASTS

Here are some examples: "To Mike Currier—one of our organization's greatest presidents. I tried to convince Mike to stay on as president for another year, but he said he is following the advice of the great philosopher Yogi Berra who said, "When you come to a fork in the road, take it."

"To Mark Bilbrey—a self-made man—and as you can tell he found it difficult to get parts."

"To Mark Korman—I have taken great liberties with you. I have kidded you, taunted you, and insulted you, but I feel I can do it with a guy like you because you have very little idea of what is going on."

Mike, Mark and Mark are three of the most gifted public speakers I have ever had the honor to hear and I knew they wouldn't take offence. They are men of conviction and humor who take the time to prepare for their talks because they respect their audiences.

I made a big mistake when I was asked to participate in a roast a number of years ago. I put together three minutes of one-liners borrowed from a book on roasts. I did not use items specific to the roastee and just went for the humor. It was a mistake, a big mistake. The audience lost their interest, and I ended up insulting the roastee. Now, I know that during a typical roast the roastee normally gets insulted, but there is a difference between canned insults and a comment that is particular to the roastee.

12

AWARDS, DEDICATIONS, AND A FUNERAL

Here is a sample award presentation I made for Mark Korman of Lancaster, Pennsylvania, in 2005 when he was presented with the highest honor in the title insurance industry. These words could be used in any industry for any major award winner:

"When I was asked to give this presentation I was torn as to which road to take. My normal inclination is to take the comedic path, but because of the seriousness of this award I felt that comedy was inappropriate. So I decided to take the more serious, editorial path.

Our industry is being challenged. Our customers want our fees cut; our policyholders question our very worth with treats of self-insurance. Legislators don't understand our business, which leaves our cries for help and protection to fall on deaf, un-understanding ears. The press takes our bad apples, of which there are some, and paints a broad brush across our entire industry.

What our industry needs are champions. The James T. Schmidt Award celebrates just such people and our award winner tonight is just such a person.

Our award winner is a champion. This champion is proud to be in our industry. This champion takes the time to learn, but even more importantly our winner takes the time to teach. When our association asks, our champion is the first to raise a proud hand to say, "I'll do it."

When faced with naysayers, our champion is not afraid to say, "Step back, I have something to say, and you are going to listen." But our winner says it with respect and receives attention and respect in return.

Our winner is not afraid to voice a contrary opinion, yet it is always said with deference to the value of the opposite opinion. Our champion has a voice that is always heard and revered.

I don't have to read the bio of our winner tonight because it is all too familiar. I just ask you now to rise and applaud the 2005 James T. Schmidt award winner, our champion, Mark Korman."

AND THE FUNERAL

My good friend Johnnie DiMarzio, a great and funny man, recently lost his father. Dad DiMarzio and his son Johnnie loved to play golf and for many, many years played the game together. When Johnnie told me he was going to give the eulogy, I questioned whether he could actually do something so emotional. He said he had to for his father. Here are some of his words:

"Thank you all for coming here today. To see so many people would have made Dad proud. We all grieve and mourn in our own way, for it is the initial step toward healing. I often choose humor to help me with my pain. So I ask you for the next few moments not to mourn the death of my father but to celebrate his life.

The last time Dad and I played golf, it was in a father-and-son tournament in June of 2002 at Pine Hill Country Club. We played together off and on for over thirty-five years.

Dad had the good fortune to play some of the finest golf courses known to man: Pebble Beach, Spyglass, Poppy Hills, Doral, Pine Valley, Mid Ocean, St. Andrews, Troon, and Carnoustie, to name a few.

My only regret is that he never got to play August National, the home of the Masters. But I know that God is a good God and that there is an Augusta National in Heaven. I am pretty sure that Dad is playing in a tournament there next week.

I just hope it's not a father-and-son tournament."

13

GAFFS, BLUNDERS, WHAT TO DO IF YOU...

TRIP ON THE WAY TO THE PODIUM—Yes, it has happened to me more times than I wish to admit. What do you do? You laugh, shake you head, get to the microphone, and tell them that your middle name is Grace. Just make light of it, and the audiences has already warmed to you.

LOSE YOUR TRAIN OF THOUGHT—I guarantee that this will happen. But think about the things you have already read in this book. If you have prepared, your mind is relaxed, and a relaxed mind will get you through any predicament. If your mind is not relaxed, you will panic.

When I lose my train of thought, I stop, look at the audience, and say something like: "My mind not only wanders, it sometimes leaves completely." Or I will say, "I bet this never happens to you, but I just forgot what I was about to say." Because it happens to everyone, you will get a great laugh. Then look at your notes or your slides, and move on to the next point. Tell them that, when the thought that you were going to expound wanders back into your brain, you will be sure to share it.

USE THE WRONG CITY OR COMPANY NAME—Don't. This is not an error that is easily erased. If necessary, write the name on a card and keep it in front of you on the podium. If you are worried about doing this, use generic terms such as "this town" or "this company."

A JOKE THAT BOMBS—Johnny Carson was better at handling a joke that bombs than any other person I have ever seen. He would just stand there and look at the audience. At times he would repeat the punch line, tap on the microphone to see if it was working, and then without saying another word he would move on.

WHEN A CELL PHONE RINGS—In the beginning of your talk, you will ask the audience to put their phones on vibrate, but invariably someone forgets or some people are just too important to be out of touch. When I hear a phone ring, sometimes I will say hello and keep on with my point. At other times, I will stop and look at the person and say, "Do you want me to get that?" with a smile on my face. They usually get the point.

If you are comfortable doing this, tell the group that if a phone rings the person has to donate $10 to the organization's PAC or pick a local charity. If a phone rings you stop and walk over to the person with your hand out and a smile on your face. I have seen this technique work beautifully.

WHEN NO ONE ANSWERS YOUR QUESTION—Let's say you are talking about handling customers who have a complaint. You pose the following question, "On average, how many people does an angry customer tell about the poor service they received?" If you do not get an answer and the audience is big enough, you simply look toward one side of the room, and, as if someone said the answer, you say, "That's right, five." If the audience is small, then answer the question yourself by raising your hand, calling on yourself, giving the answer, and complimenting yourself for the correct answer.

WHAT IF I RUN OUT OF MATERIAL—If you have completed the three steps outlined in this book, you know that one of the reasons we practice our talks out loud is to get the timing correct. But stuff happens. You may be asked to stretch your talk until the next speaker, who is running late, gets there. I always have extra material in the way a quiz. Put together a few screens or questions about the material you have covered in your talk—just in case. Throw in a few funny questions that have no relevancy but will kill some time and bring a few smiles.

> Name the Seven Wonders of the World—and have your audience work in twosomes.
> What are the capitals of the thirteen original states? What are the thirteen original states?
> What are the best customer service commercials on TV today?

Ray Didinger, a phenomenal sportswriter, author, and football expert with NFL Films, said on 610WIP Sports Talk Radio in May of 2005, a true professional "finishes every game with his uniform dirty." I don't think he meant that we need to fall to the ground, but I think he means that if you consider yourself a professional the effort must be there no matter what happens.

14

A BANG-UP ENDING

You had a good opening, a good middle, and now it is time to leave a final impression. For technical talks you can simply end with a compliment for your audience, saying something like, "Thanks for bearing with me; thanks for paying attention; thanks for not falling asleep. I'll stick around if you have any additional questions, but make them easy because my brain is as fried as yours."

For motivational endings, I have ended many speeches with a motivating and moving story that bring tears to the audience every time. It takes at least ten minutes to tell this moving story if it is told properly and with feeling. This story gets a very strong point across, while pulling at the heartstrings of men, women and children alike. I have ended many, many speeches with the famous "Jimmy" story and in never fails to bring tears to the audience and to me each and every time. You need to find your own "Jimmy" story but I have included mine at the end of this book.

It will not be hard to find your own story with the plethora of e-mails we receive every day about people who have done something wonderful. People send me many good stories, and I always print them out and put them in a file. Someday I may be able to use one. Don't save everything, just the best.

But you need to make the story your own by…you guessed it…practicing it out loud, over and over again until you can tell it by heart, pause at the appropriate moments and emphasize the right words to get your point across. The most important thing to remember is that the story must fit in with the message of your talk; otherwise it will seem like a cheap add-on, and it will only detract from your speech.

15

THE POST GAME

I have always thought about the psyche of professional athletes when it comes to the post game. True professionals care about winning and losing. and think about it, after a win they feel successful; however, after a loss, how do they feel? The true professional has the choice of only two emotions—elation and defeat—at the end of each game, each match, each race. There is nothing in between.

A sports fan cheers for his or her team after wins, but the true fan also cheers when his or her team loses *if* the players display the three Ps: preparation, practice, and presentation. A true sports fan applauds when the effort is stellar but abhors any lack of effort. If a player truly tries, if a player truly cares, and gives his or her all, a true sports fan is satisfied and remains a fan even in the face of a defeat.

I have a friend who is a fan when the local teams are winning, claiming that team to be *his* team. But the minute those teams fail he declares that they are "bums." My friend is not a *true* sports fan. Even in the face of a loss, if the players and coaches on my team gave everything they had, they can never be bums. In other words, they got their uniforms dirty in the effort. If they made mistakes, maybe they weren't as mentally gifted as their opponents. If they were beat physically, maybe they weren't as physically strong as their opponents—but that does not make them bums. It just makes the other team the better team on that given day, but I am still a fan because they tried. They showed me that they cared enough to prepare, practice, and then they performed, as best as they could.

If my team or any of the players on that team show a lack of effort, a lack of caring, or an apathetic attitude towards preparation, then they do not deserve my "fan-dom" or loyalty. And I will let them know that, not through boos, never through boos, but through intelligently articulated communication. But, if they prepared to the best of their ability, practiced to the best of their ability, and performed to the best of their ability, they are deemed successful by the *true* fans of the world.

When speaking in front of an audience, you must remember that 99.9 percent of people listening and watching will be true fans *if* you have prepared, practiced, and then presented to the best of your ability. What else in life can guarantee you a 99.9 percent chance that people will support you?

This book has given you steps to increase your rate of success by helping you prepare and insisting that you practice. Audiences are astute when it comes to recognizing a speaker who has not taken the task seriously and is not prepared. They can spot it in a New York minute, which I just learned is the amount of time between the light turning green and the driver behind you blowing the horn in New York City. If you prepare well, if you practice hard, you cannot fail because your audience will recognize your effort.

FINAL WORDS

I understand that if you are nervous about speaking no one can tell you not to be. My hope is that this book has given you a number of methods that will help you relax a bit—by preparing a lot.

Here are a few phrases that fit at this moment as we talk about our need to overcome our fears:

"No pain no gain." You may be afraid, but look at what a good speech will do for you. You will be proud of yourself, recognize that you worked hard to prepare, and others will respect you for what you said and how you said it.

Thomas Paine once said, "The harder the conflict, the more glorious the triumph. What we obtain too cheap, we esteem too lightly." The sense of accomplishment and the rush of adrenalin you will feel after doing a good job is similar to a great sports win, a hard workout, or solving a tough, tough problem. You know how hard you worked and you are exhausted, but it hurts so good.

16

THE BEST ENDING STORY IN THE HISTORY OF MANKIND

I heard this story on a cassette tape many, many years ago and cannot for the life of me remember whose tape it was or who the story was about. Perhaps someone reading this book will call me and tell me. It is one of the best motivational endings I have ever heard. When told properly, it will take a good ten minutes to tell, but it holds an audience spellbound.

"It was 1935 in Smalltown, USA. In the town lived a woman by the name of Lady Jones. Now the townspeople did not know if she was royalty, but she spoke with a British accent and owned the largest home in town, so they called her Lady Jones.

Lady Jones told all of the children in the town that they could not cut through her yard. One day little Jimmy was late. He was always late, but he thought that if he cut through Lady Jones's backyard he could get home faster and not be in so much trouble.

He came up to the back of the house and looked over the fence to see if he could see Lady Jones. He did not. He hopped over the fence and nervously started running across the back of Lady Jones's yard.

From around the corner of the house came Lady Jones.

"Say, you son, didn't I tell you children not to cross my lawn?"

"Yes, ma'am, Lady Jones, I am so sorry," Jimmy said nervously. Jimmy was scared.

"Wait a moment, aren't you Jimmy from down the street?" asked Lady Jones.

"Yes, ma'am. I'm so sorry."

"Don't I see you cutting your lawn every Saturday?"

"Yes, ma'am. I'm so sorry."

Lady Jones paused for a second and then said, "I want you to be my gardener."

"Yes, ma'am. I'm so sorry. What?" asked a puzzled Jimmy.

"I want you to be my gardener."

"Yes, ma'am. Whatever you want, ma'am," replied Jimmy. You see, when Lady Jones asked for something, the people just naturally did what she requested.

"Well, Jimmy, don't you want to know how it will work?" asked Lady Jones.

"Sure," said a bewildered Jimmy.

"Here's the deal Jimmy: The $1.00 job will not be good enough. The $1.00 job is a job where I would have to supervise you constantly, you would never get it right, and you would take too much of my time. I would have to fire you. The $2.00 job still is not good enough. I would have to supervise you, eventually you would get it right, but it would still waste my time and I would have to fire you. The $3.00 job is just average. No more, no less than any boy your age would do. Now the $4.00 job, Jimmy, is special, because that is where you show initiative. You do things without my asking, and you go beyond my expectations. The $5.00 job, Jimmy, is for the best. The $5.00 job is for people who put in all kinds of time. Their friends think they are crazy for working so hard. It is a job only for those who want to be the best. But Jimmy, looking at you, I can tell that you can't relate to the $5.00 job."

"No, ma'am," replied Jimmy. "I ain't never seen $5.00."

You have to remember that this is 1935. A nickel bought a loaf of bread. For a dime Jimmy could spend the day and eat three meals at the picture show. His family, though not destitute, could live well from this job.

"OK, Jimmy, I will see you next week," said Lady Jones as she turned to go.

All of the way home, Jimmy was thinking about the money. He was imagining what he was going to do with all of that money.

The next week he went to Lady Jones's house. He cut the lawn. He saw the weeds in the garden, but she didn't ask him to pull them. He knocked on the door when he was finished, and Lady Jones asked, "Are you finished, Jimmy?"

"Yes, ma'am," said Jimmy.

"Well, Jimmy, what are you worth?" she asked.

"What do you mean, ma'am?" questioned Jimmy.

"Remember when I told you about the deal? What are you worth?" she repeated.

"I don't rightly know, ma'am. No one has ever asked me that before," Jimmy said.

"Well, just this once, Jimmy, I am going to help you," she said. So down the steps they went. Lady Jones saw that the front lawn was cut, but there were patches that Jimmy had missed. She saw the weeds in the garden, but she had not asked him to pull them; she saw the leaves that could have been raked but were not; and she saw that the backyard wasn't cut at all.

Jimmy was embarrassed. He hurriedly finished the cutting and raked the leaves and a bit later he knocked on her door. "Are you finished, Jimmy?" Lady Jones asked. "Yes, ma'am," Jimmy replied meekly. Lady Jones handed him $3.00.

"Frankly, Jimmy," she said, "you are not worth $3.00, but I am going to give it to you anyway. I'll see you next week.

She turned to go back into the house, and, as if speaking to herself but loud enough for Jimmy to hear, she said, "When I hired him, I thought at least he would be average, but I have been wrong before," and, boom, she shut the door.

Jimmy was angry. He'd show her! Next week he would cut the lawn, rake the leaves, and cut the back, and when she went to hand him $3.00, he would give her a dollar back because this week she had overpaid him and he wouldn't be beholden to anyone.

The next week Jimmy went to Lady Jones's house and cut the lawn. He saw the weeds in the garden, but she hadn't asked him to pull them; he raked the leaves and he cut the back lawn. He then knocked on Lady Jones's door. Rap, rap, rap.

"Are you finished, Jimmy?" asked Lady Jones.

"Yes, ma'am," replied Jimmy.

"Well, what are you worth?"

"Three dollars, Lady Jones, but you only owe me two," said Jimmy.

"What do you mean, Jimmy?"

"I did the $3.00 job, but last week you overpaid me, and I won't be beholden to no one," said Jimmy proudly.

Lady Jones smiled and, as she inspected the job, she saw that indeed he had done a $3.00 job. When they returned to the front step, she handed Jimmy $3.00, and, as Jimmy started to hand her a dollar back, she said, "No, Jimmy, you keep this extra dollar, and when you go home I want you to put it in a frame and write the word 'integrity' under it because that is what you've got. See you next week."

She turned to go back into the house, and, as if speaking to herself but loudly enough for Jimmy to hear, she said, "Gee, when I hired him I thought he would be special, but I have been wrong before," and, boom, she shut the door.

Jimmy was angry. His mother thought he was special; his grandfather thought he was special. But then he remembered his first conversation with Lady Jones. She had told him that to do the $4.00 job, the special job, you had to show initiative. You had to go above and beyond.

On his way home, Jimmy stopped at the library. "Mrs. Librarian, do you know what 'initiative' means?"

"Why yes, Jimmy," said the librarian. "It means doing something extra without being asked. It means going above and beyond."

"Well, I am Lady Jones's gardener. I cut the grass. I rake the leaves. What else can I do?" he asked.

"Jimmy, we have a book on gardening. Would you like to read it?" she said as she smiled.

"You bet," said Jimmy with a grin.

He opened the book, and guess what the first chapter told him to do...pull the weeds. Then Jimmy read about edging the lawn and trimming the bushes. So the next week he told his mother he would be late for dinner because he had a lot of work to do.

Jimmy got to Lady Jones's house and he cut the lawn, he raked the leaves, he trimmed the bushes, he edged the lawn, and then he pulled the weeds. It took him as long to pull the weeds as it did everything else. And at the end of a long afternoon, he walked up the front steps and knocked on the door. Rap, rap, rap.

"Why, Jimmy, you have been here a long time."

"Yes, ma'am. It's a big job."

"Well, Jimmy, what are you worth?"

"Four dollars, ma'am. I'm special," said Jimmy proudly.

"You are, are you? Let's go see." And down the steps they went. Lady Jones saw that he had cut the lawn, trimmed the bushed, edged the grass, raked the leaves, and pulled the weeds. They climbed the front steps, and Lady Jones said, while handing Jimmy $4.00, "Jimmy, you are indeed special. You showed initiative and went above and beyond my expectations. You can be very proud of yourself. Then she paused and added, "But of course it's not the best."

Jimmy was crestfallen.

"Jimmy, remember when I told you that the $5.00 job was for the best? You have to put in all kinds of hours, and your friends will think you are crazy. You can be very satisfied with being special. I will see you next week." And into the house she went, smiling widely, leaving Jimmy on the front step with a startled look on his face.

After he cooled off, he started to think about what she had said. To be the best she had told him he had to put in so much extra time. His friends would think he was crazy.

As Jimmy walked home, he realized that he wasn't the best at anything. He wasn't the best student; he wasn't the best baseball player; and he wondered what it would be like, for once in his life, to be the best at something, anything.

So he stopped at the library again the next day, and he picked up where he left off in the book on gardening. He read the chapter about cutting the lawn in two different directions to get the checkerboard effect. He read the chapter on how to trim the bushes into shapes, and then he read the chapter on pruning the roses. He knew that Lady Jones's most prized possession in her garden were her roses, and he also knew that she was dreading the day when she would have to spend her time pruning.

The next week he told his mother that he would be leaving before dawn to go to Lady Jones's and that she should not hold dinner because he would be coming home late—he had a big job to do.

Jimmy cut the lawn once and then cut it again in a different direction. His friends rode by on their bikes and said, "Hey, Jimmy, are you crazy? You already cut the lawn!"

Jimmy just smiled to himself because he remembered that Lady Jones told him people would think he was crazy if he worked hard enough to be the best. Then he raked the leaves, pulled the weeds, shaped the bushes, and then set to work pruning the roses.

Very late in the afternoon, a tired Jimmy knocked on Lady Jones's door. Rap, rap, rap.

"My, Jimmy, you are here late today. Are you finished?"

"Yes, ma'am."

"What are you worth today?"

"Five dollars. I'm the best," Jimmy said proudly.

"Oh, Jimmy, you must mean $4.00 because you're special."

"No, ma'am. Five dollars because I'm the best. Come and see."

They went down the front steps, and Lady Jones saw her lawn. "My oh my, Jimmy! I haven't seen a lawn look this beautiful since I left England."

She saw that he had raked the leaves, pulled the weeds, trimmed the bushes, and out of the corner of her eye she saw her roses and she started to cry. And Jimmy started to cry.

"Jimmy, what ever possessed you to do such a wonderful thing?" she asked quietly.

"Lady Jones, I knew you were dreading the day you would have to prune your roses...and I just wondered what it would feel like, just once in my life, to be the best."

She took a moment and looked down at Jimmy and said, "How does it feel?"

"It feels wonderful. But when you started to cry, I realized that it wasn't the money. It is the pride I feel in myself at this moment."

This is a true story. Jimmy grew up to be the CEO of a Fortune 500 company, and until his retirement in the 70s, whenever Jimmy was asked to what he attributed his success he always said, "Lady Jones." Because she taught him, "A job paid for a job done." She taught him the meaning of the word "integrity," and more importantly she taught him what it took and felt like to be the best.

The best endings are based on truth. After a customer service speech where I explain that simple human decency creates the best customer relations, I tell this true story.

I was getting gas one day and noticed an older woman doing the same at the pump next to me. She was beautifully dressed and her hair was done to perfection, but she looked distracted and lost. She passed me to pay the attendant, and I told her how pretty she looked.

She started to cry.

Then she walked over to me and told me that she had recently lost her husband of sixty years, and today was the first day she had left the house without him after all of those years. She told me that my kind words would give her the courage to come out of her house again tomorrow.

I am reaching for a tissue as I relate this, but it shows you that a kind word, a courteous gesture, and human warmth will help you make wonderful presentations and give your audience a reason to stand and cheer.

978-0-595-38305-4
0-595-38305-X

CPSIA information can be obtained
at www.ICGtesting.com
Printed in the USA
BVHW07s0319280918
528720BV00001B/26/P